Crime in Bedfordshire in John Bunyan's Day

1660 – 1688

By

Evelyn Curtis

eBook version September 2012

978-1-909667-08-2 - Mobi
978-1-909667-09-9 - eBook-ePub
978-1-909667-10-5 - Paperback

Published by Hob Hill Books
www.hobhill.com

CONTENTS

INTRODUCTION

This account is drawn mainly from existing records of the Bedfordshire Assizes during the Restoration period. These records number over a thousand documents and include statements made by accused persons and witnesses taken down verbatim before a Justice of the Peace, recognisances binding witnesses and accused to appear in court, bills of presentment recording the names of the accused and their alleged offences, with a note of sentence passed, and lists of prisoners in the County Gaol. The whole gives a detailed picture of crime, trial and punishment in the seventeenth century Assize courts, revealing incidentally many aspects of the social life of the time. The Assize records are of particular value because only one Indictment book, covering the years 1651 to 1660, has survived of the Bedfordshire Quarter Sessions records which should provide similar material.

THE ASSIZES

The county of Bedfordshire formed part of the old Norfolk Assize circuit. Twice a year, in February and in August, two judges on circuit from the courts at Westminster arrived in Bedfordshire with power to try all treasons, felonies and misdemeanors committed in the county, and also to examine any prisoner in the County Gaol. The High Sheriff convened the Assizes, and summoned Justices of the Peace, Bailiffs of Liberties and Hundreds, Coroners and Chief Constables to attend. At the beginning of the Assizes all bills of presentment were examined by the Grand Jury, which had power to stop proceedings if it found there was no case to be answered, after which the prisoner would be discharged by proclamation. The prisoners who were indicted would be tried by the Petty Jury, and proceedings in court were similar to those at a Modern Assize. Felons would be tried first, then those summoned for trespass and misdemeanor.

PUNISHMENT

The frequency of capital punishment is the most striking feature of the sentences passed. Treason and all felony except petty larceny were punishable by death, and petty larceny meant the theft of goods worth only 12 pence. or under, an amount retained owing to the conservatism of the law, for the value of money had decreased since earlier centuries. The rigor of the law was mitigated, however, by the grant of benefit of clergy, which reduced the sentence to branding in the hand. Persons convicted of certain felonies might plead benefit of clergy if they could read from a book presented to them, a survival from the time when book-learning was confined to the clergy, who were exempt from capital punishment. Benefit of clergy was not abolished until 1822, but by the seventeenth century it had been taken away from the gravest offences, such as murder, robbing of houses and horse stealing. Other punishments imposed included transportation to the plantations of America, Barbados or Jamaica, branding in the hand or face,

6

whipping, and of course the imposition of fines. The stocks and pillory were appointed as punishments for certain offences. Imprisonment was not often decreed as a sentence, except for political prisoners, and for those like John Bunyan, imprisoned for their religious principles. Sometimes, however, a prisoner might lie in gaol for as long as five years, awaiting transportation, and others stayed there because they could not pay their fines.

THE GAOLS

There were two prisons in Bedford in the seventeenth century, the County Gaol on a site at the north-west corner of the junction of Silver Street and the High Street, and the smaller Town Gaol on Bedford Bridge. There was also a Bridewell, or House of Correction, in Cauldwell Street. It was to the County Gaol that most prisoners to be tried at the Assizes were sent. The conditions in gaol were probably as bad as those John Howard described a century later; Bunyan, who was imprisoned in the County Gaol for twelve years, wrote that sooner than violate his principles he would stay there 'till the moss should grow upon his eyebrows'. The difficulty of keeping prisoners in disease-ridden and insecurely guarded prisons was one reason why the death penalty was imposed so often.

The Assize records show that several attempts were made to escape from Bedford County Gaol. In 1684 Richard Butler, a yeoman of Bedford,was charged with bringing a file, hammer, chisel and punch into the gaol to help three prisoners committed for robbery to cut their fetters.

The escape was planned for the night when the gaolkeeper was away at Ampthill for the Assizes. One of the prisoners in the plot, however, confessed to the gaolkeeper's wife. Butler pleaded guilty at his trial and was fined £50. The Grand Jury in 1688 dismissed the case against Grace West of Bedford on a similar charge of bringing files, knives and other instruments to enable a prisoner to escape. In 1673 the then gaolkeeper was charged with allowing a man imprisoned for illegally collecting hearth-tax money to go free. In 1666 his predecessor was indicted at the Assizes for assaulting one Thomas Collard, and for corruptly receiving money from him, but the case was dismissed.

CRIMINAL CASES

Of the crimes brought before the Assize judges theft of property is of course the most common horses, cattle and sheep stealing, highway robbery, picking pockets, poaching and much burglary and housebreaking, for houses and shops were poorly protected against the burglar. In twenty eight years, thirty three murder charges are recorded, but many of these were reduced to manslaughter. There is one case of coining, for which a man was hanged. Witchcraft remained an indictable offence until the repeal of the statute of James I in 1736, and during our period there is evidence of four witchcraft trials at Bedford, but no conviction is recorded.

MURDER AND ASSAULT

In 1678 a quarrel on the road to Luton,in which two men riding with a loaded horse had refused to make way for a party of people led to the conviction of one of the men for murder, at the Assizes.

He had been struck with a whip and had pulled the man who had struck him off his horse and had beaten him to death. At the trial he was found guilty, pleaded benefit of clergy and was branded. Another assault was made by a shoemaker of Sutton, who saw a soldier chasing a chicken on his ground and in anger gave the thief a blow on the head, from which he died. The shoemaker was indicted at the Assizes in 1679.

John Winch, a labourer, was brought to trial in 1680 after a brawl in the widow Chapman's blacksmith's shop in Luton. Winch haid said to one Thomas Crawley 'Heer's the Rogue that works for eight pence a day, when others have twelve pence'. Crawley replied 'You lye you old Rogue - I have 10d'. After more talk with oathes on both sides ... the said John Winch being lightinge a pipe of Tabacco with an iron rod being red hott, did run the same into the Eye of the said Thomas Crawley, and told him that he would teach him to stare in his face'. Winch pleaded guilty and was fined £100.

In 1671 Thomas Carter was branded for killing Oliver Brownall, a butcher's apprentice, with a pitchfork. The butcher had hired Carter and his servants Hannaway and Lee to move dung out of his yard, but the apprentice played about and hindered their work, until Cartier in exasperation threw a fork at him. It hit him on the head and he died a few weeks later. Carter, his servants and the butcher's wife all gave evidence that the fork had been aimed at Brownall's legs, but he had bent down just as it came. In 1676 a labourer was tried for the murder of a fellow-workman whose leg he had accidentally cut while scything in a field, but the charge was reduced to manslaughter.

At Eaton Socon in 1680 there was an attempted murder at the house of a yeoman, William Barcocke. One of the servants, William Welbye, attempted to kill a fellow-servant, Thomas Merrill. Welbye had made a hole in the roof above Merrill's Chamber, had let himself down and had cut Merrill's throat as he lay in bed at night. Only the arrival of the mistress of the house and the maid, who had seen a light and thought there was a fire, saved Merrill's life. As they reached the door of the room Welbye rushed out. They found Merrill seriously wounded, crying 'Where is Welbye?'. The light had been caused by a candle put on a beam in the roof beside the hole. At the next Assizes Welbye was found guilty of breaking into William Barcocke's house at night with intent to murder Thomas Merrill and to steal his property. He was sentenced to be hanged.

In 1682 a quarrel in the street at Tempsford over the possession of a knife led to the trial of Edward Adey and his wife for the murder of Rose Webb but witnesses gave conflicting evidence of the cause of her death; some said a head wound, others that Adey had kicked her. The depositions in this case show the general ignorance of medical matters at this time; illness and injury, moreover, received little or no attention among the poor, and when death followed the most unlikely causes were found for it. A little boy died a week after being frightened by a dog, and although there was no evidence of a bite, the dog's master was prosecuted at the Assizes, where the case was rightly dismissed. Sometimes an unexplained death would be attributed to the 'spells and enchantments' of a witch.

WITCHCRAFT

Though sceptics doubted, the belief in witchcraft was widespread. For over a century England had suffered from outbreaks of witch-hunting fever, the last of these being the prosecutions and mob violence during the Civil War associated with the name of Matthew Hopkins, lawyer of Ipswich and 'witchfinder general'.

After the Restoration witch-hunting, always more prevalent among the Puritans, died hard. Sir Matthew Hale, (1609-1676), justice of the common pleas in 1654, who rose to be Lord Chief Justice in 1671, stated his belief in witchcraft 'as affirmed by the Scriptures', at a trial at Bury St. Edmunds in 1665, when he sentenced two women to be hanged. Hale was Assize judge on the Norfolk circuit and sat at Bedford at least fifteen times between 1660 and 1674. It is likely, however, that other judges were becoming less willing to convict for witchcraft. The last recorded execution in England was at Exeter in 1685.

There are four witchcraft trials in the Assize records for Bedfordshire, three of them between 1662 and 1669, the fourth later, in 1680. No conviction is recorded. The first case is that of Richard Favell, a shepherd of Stagsden, and Mary Favell, spinster, perhaps his daughter or sister, who were to be prosecuted at the Winter Assizes in 1662. They were allowed bail, but no presentment exists, and the outcome of their trial,if it took place, is not known. In the spring of 1667 a remarkable case came before the judges Sir Wadham Wyndham and Sir William Morton. The episode began the year before, when four Dunstable women had been accused of witchcraft,the most serious charge being that of bewitching small children to death. First, Elizabeth Pratt, a widow, had been brought before two justices of the peace as a witch, and the two women appointed to search her had found witches' marks on her body. Elizabeth had in her turn accused three of her neighbours, Mary Poole, an innkeeper's wife, Ursula Clarke, the wife of a labourer, and Mary Hudson, a butcher's wife, of causing the sickness of the two children of Thomas Heywood, which she herself denied. She admitted, however, that the Devil had appeared to her - in three forms as a man, a woman and a cat. On his command she had met the three women she was accusing at the three knolls on Dunstable downs, where they had cursed the children, but she had taken no part in the cursing. Another, time the Devil had ordered her to curse William Metcalfe's cattle, because he called her witch; she had done so, and he was to assert that sixty five horses - probably post horses in a coaching stable - and seventeen hogs, worth together £510, had died as the result. He said that he was in his yard, with the doors and gates shut, when Elizabeth Pratt appeared, and when asked how she got in she told him she came through the keyhole. Other witnesses said that the widow Pratt had said that 'George Heywood his back was her pannell to ryde on, and she had ridden him up hill and down hill'. The Devil had made a contract with her, promising that she should live as well as the best woman in Dunstable, 'but that now she found him a lyer'. She said that there were twenty witches in Dunstable that wore better clothes than she, but she would not reveal any of them yet.

The three that she had revealed denied everything. Most of the accusations against them depended on her testimony; for example, Thomas Heywood's wife had found a knot of black wool tied to the sick child's bolster, and Elizabeth Pratt said Mary Hudson had put it there. Other witnesses, however, gave evidence of a quarrel between Ursula Clarke and William Metcalfe, in which Ursula had said 'she hoped to see him ... waste like dew against the sun'. Mary Hudson had once said she wished one Crawley of Houghton Regis would break his neck, 'which happened indeed for he fell from his horse'.

There is no evidence of any prosecution at the Assizes that year, but in September a further charge was made against Elizabeth Pratt, that some eighteen months before she had caused the deaths of John and Josias, the sons of Josias Settle, a barber-surgeon. She had come to the Settles' house 'begging ale and toast' and had stroked John's head, saying that the two brothers were her boys. Two days later John 'was took with a strange distemper, groaning and crying continually until he died ... and crying 'Murder, murder, I am bewitched'. Two weeks later the elder brother fell sick and cried 'The widow Pratt has bewitched me'. At this neighbours fetched the unfortunate Elizabeth Pratt, and an unpleasant scene followed, in which they forced the boy to scratch her with a pin,and true to the popular belief about witches he could not make her bleed.

As a result of these accusations,Elizabeth Pratt, Mary Hudson and Ursula Clarke were ordered to appear at the next Assizes in the spring of 1667. Mary and Ursula were allowed bail, but Elizabeth was sent to the County Gaol, to await the Assizes. Before the time came she had died in prison. With the death of the only self- confessed witch of the three the alarm in Dunstable seems to have died down. By a coincidence (or the malevolence of the witches) both Heywood and Settle, two of the accusers, died just after the Assizes. The only trial of which there is evidence is that of Mary Hudson, charged with causing the death of John

Heywood by witchcraft, and she was found not guilty. She appears to have lived on in Dunstable until her death in 1675.

There is a footnote to the Dunstable witchcraft episode in the Assize records for 1678, when one Daniel Hudson, perhaps Mary's husband, was acquitted of the charge of setting fire to stacks of straw, pease, barley and oats belonging to one Thomas Groome. One of the witnesses against Hudson was William Metcalfe, yeoman of Dunstable.

A similar witchcraft case occurred in 1669, when Ellin Inch of Woburn was acquitted of the charge of bewitching a small boy, but no witnesses' statements survive. The last trial is that of John Wright of Bedford in 1680. A bricklayer's wife in the parish of St. Peter Merton, Dinah Wiffin, was subject to fits of madness, and became obsessed with the memory of a beggar she had turned away from her door, one John Wright, who is described as a shoemaker. Her family seized on her tale of Wright appearing to her in dreams and threatening her; it was plain that he had bewitched her and caused her madness. Wright was brought before the mayor of Bedford. He appeared bewildered. 'Being demanded whether he was a witch (he) said he did not know but he trust to God he is not'. However, he seemed to be able to forecast the time and course of Dinah's fits, and, according to her brother, he had at one point actually confessed to bewitching her, and he had said that Goody Morgan of Goldington had joined with him. Wright was sent to the Town Gaol. At the next Assizes he stood trial on the charge that he bewitched Dinah Wiffin 'so that she pined and wasted away' and was acquitted.

CHILDREN AT THE ASSIZES

Children appear frequently in the Assize records. The death of an illegitimate child at birth brought the mother under suspicion of murder, if the birth was discovered. A child found dead from exposure would lead to the indictment of the mother or nurse who abandoned it, like the woman who left a child in a field one morning, 'perceiving some maids coming to milk'. The parish overseers made her take it back, but it died later that day. Children might stand trial at the Assizes. Michael Merrill, a poor boy was sentenced to be whipped in 1669 for stealing twelve brass farthings, probably trade tokens, out of a money box belonging to a Shefford grocer. In 1678 a boy named John Harper was branded for breaking open a mercer's shop at Clophill and stealing three knives, two tobacco boxes, some whipcord and half an ounce of tobacco. He was found hiding under a hedge with the stolen goods.

A child of eight, Sylvanus Simpson, was brought to trial, and fortunately acquitted, for killing John Taylor, a little boy of the same age, at Maulden in 1672. Sylvanus had accidentally discharged a handgun which he had picked up in his father's yard. His mother, in the house, heard a shot, and John Taylor fell down beside her. She found her son outside crying 'indeed mother and I did not know the gun was charged'. A servant boy who was with a man shooting sparrows had been killed when he had taken hold of the man's gun, shouting 'shoot me, shoot me!'. and plucking the cock of the gun. It went off, and the game ended in tragedy. In 1688 a quarrel between Francis Sharpe aged fourteen and James Lyne aged nine, in which Francis knocked James on the head with an ash club and pushed him into a pond, led to Francis' trial for murder. He was found guilty, pleaded benefit of clergy and was branded.

There is the pathetic story of Sarah Mosse, aged ten, a pauper apprentice put out by the town of Houghton Conquest, and found drowned in a pond. Her master and mistress, Thomas and Elizabeth Willimott, were found not guilty of the murder at the Assizes. The evidence was that Elizabeth had never wanted to take the child, and that once she had flung her downstairs for falling asleep after being called in the morning. Sarah had been seen barefoot driving cows, but 'she had good wheaten bread and cheese to eat' and had been heard oftentimes merry and singing when her dame hath been abroad'. Rumours that Sarah was ill-treated had got about, and the town offered to take her back, if Willimott would return the 50 shillings paid to him, which he refused to do. Other witnesses said that Sarah was well provided for, but the goodwife Mosse, her stepmother, had said she wished Sarah might drown herself so that the goodwife Willimot might suffer, Then Sarah disappeared, going away about candlelight one evening. The Willimott children said she had crept out by the orchard door, and she was not seen alive again.

MASTERS AND SERVANTS

There are many cases concerning masters and servants, usually dishonest servants. A silver cup disappeared mysteriously from a bench in the yard of an inn at Woburn, and one maidservant suspected another. At St. Neots a gardener stole materials from the shop of his employer, a mercer, whose suspicions were aroused when he heard the gardener's wife had sold stuffs in Bedford for a very low price. A servant of Lady, St. John at Tempsford stole £14 and some clothes from the chest of Lady St, John's bailiff. He got as far as Shefford, and said he intended to go to London had he not been stopped. In 1671 William Norton, a travelling player on the pipe and drum, and Sarah Spencer, a maid at a Shefford Inn, were accused of stealing linen articles from the inn. Their escape before daybreak was discovered by Norton's wife and they were pursued to Holwell. Norton said he had bidden Sarah take nothing but her own but she told a different story. 'The said Will told hyr that he wold give hyr ten pounds to leave hyr place and goe with him and that he wold carrye hyr into a brave country and where shee shold live braveley and that hee wold buye hyr new clothes and marry hyr and that upon hys enticing of hyr shee did goe awaye with hym and carryed awaye some small parcells of linnen which weare the goods of Marye Farre hyr dame'. They pleaded guilty and were whipped at the Assize.

THEFT AND HOUSEBREAKING

House and shopbreaking were very common. Thieves might get in while the family was away, or at chirch, and take whatever lay to hand. In 1673 Thomas Eastwell, a labourer, was accused of stealing a pair of trousers ('subligaculi anglice Trousers'), a shirt, two bands (collars), a pair of stockings and some money from the house of Richard Harries, a Tempsford butcher. Eastwell confessed that he had taken the key of the house from a neighbour while the butcher was away, and had gone inside to look for weights to borrow for weighing cheeses. This story was not believed by the butcher, who said that Eastwell 'was well known in the said town to be a pilfering theevish fellow'.

John Newland, a carpenter of Ampthill broke into a house while the family was at church on Christmas Day 1680, and stole £6.17.6d from a trunk. On being arrested, he said that one John Sandy had been with him, and that they had decided to steal money 'for they were to have a great Cocking the next day', i.e. a cockfight with betting.

In 1670 Ralph Meakes, a labourer of Bedford was branded for stealing a large quantity of textiles - silk materials such as lute-string, tamerine and prunella - from a draper's shop in St. Neots. Several persons, including a linen draper and tailor, were indicted with him for receiving, but they were found not guilty. For stealing a watch which was lying on a pair of virginals in the house of William Whitbread at Cardington, Thomas Hensman, a tailor from Wellingborough, was whipped at the Summer Assizes in 1668.

There are two cases of thieves taking 'a piece of King Charles the Second his touching gold for the evell', worth 5s. These small gold coins were distributed at the ceremony by which persons suffering from the 'King's Evil' (scrofula) were touched in order to be cured by the sovereign. The coins were pierced and hung round the neck; in one of the Assize cases the thief stole the piece from the neck of a child while it slept. In 1675 a Biddenham labourer was whipped for stealing a coat, a band and 22 shillings. from George Harries of Little Gransden in Cambridgeshire, a servant, Harries told how he had been 'overtaken in drincke' one evening at Bedford, and had hired John Gale for 2d to accompany him to Bromham, but when they got to the windmill Harries lay down and slept. He woke up later to find his coat and money missed, and Gale had disappeared.

HIGHWAYMEN

In the south of the county, Watling Street, the main road to the north west from London, seems to have been much favoured by highwaymen. A coachman gave evidence in 1671 that while he was driving the stage coach between Dunstable and Hockliffe three mounted highwaymen assaulted the passengers. Afterwards the three were traced to a Stanbridge alehouse, where they defended themselves with a pistol and sword against the local constable and his helpers and wounded two of them, In the end one of the highwaymen fled, another was fatally wounded, and the third was captured and confessed. Two brothers of Leighton Buzzard were found not guilty in 1675 of stealing £9 from a man who asserted that on the road between Brick Hill in Buckinghamshire and Hockliffe and brothers 'did terrifie him very much by holding a pistoll at his breast'. In 1680 Robert Long gave evidence that two men robbed him of 3 shillings on the Woburn road, and whipped away his horse, which was found the next day at Ridgmont.

John Jenkins was hanged in 1683 for stealing 14 shillings. from John Wildes. Jenkins had beaten Wildes into a ditch beside the road, crying 'God damn you, deliver your money or else I will pistoll you'. Wildes pleaded that he was an old man and unable to fight, and gave up his purse. Jenkin put the money in his hat and returned the purse saying 'God be with you and God bless you'. In 1679 Richard Rolph and George Sole the younger of Flitwick, on the Luton to Bedford road, were charged with 'harbouring and being counsell with highwaymen'. Rolph had to give as much as £200 surety, and his brothers a further £100 each, before he was allowed bail. The witnesses in the case, including two prisoners brought from gaol, gave evidence of suspicious comings and goings at Rolph's house at Flitwick, and said that he and Sole had known the highwaymen King and Clayton,imprisoned in Newgate and later hanged.

HORSE STEALING

The theft of horses must have been as common as the theft of cars today. Fairs and markets up and down the country gave opportunity for disposing of stolen horses quickly, although we read of the owner of a stolen horse having its description 'publicly cried at Dunstable fair'. A man might find himself charged with receiving a horse he had bought in good faith from a thief; one man complained that he was arrested and would have been taken to prison, had not the Justice of the Peace before whom he was brought known him for an honest man. A thief might arouse suspicion if he offered the horse for too low a price, in order to sell it quickly. In 1678 John Taylor was acquitted of stealing a mare Humphrey Blackwall had offered for sale in Smithfield, London. Blackwall asserted that Taylor had tricked him, hesitating over the price and asking to ride her a step before deciding whether to buy. He had ridden off on the mare and had disappeared. Later Blackwall found the sale of the mare to another man recorded in the Dunstable fair tollbook.

Taylor said that he had returned with the mare to Smithfield on the same day he had met Blackwall but had been unable to find him; the Assize judge and jury seem to have believed him.

Thomas Morgan, who stole a bay gelding at Clifton, was informer as well as horse thief, for he said in evidence that he had been living in Yorkshire with Mr. Thomas Cotes, a Roman Catholic, and had been on his way to London to give evidence against certain Roman Catholics. This was during the Popish Plot scare of 1678. Morgan was sentenced to hanging, but was reprieved and transported. A labourer from Coventry, Thomas Topp, was hanged in 1684 for stealing five horses from different stables. He insisted that they had all 'been bought and tolled for', that is, he had bought each horse in the open market,and the market tolls had been paid. He said he was a poor man, nearly blind. At the next Assizes a hempdresser of Old Warden was committed to gaol for keeping company with Topp.

SHEEP STEALING

This was another common crime; there were always dishonest butchers, like John Gurney of Hockliffe, who would accept stolen sheep, and there were also the markets for disposing of them. One Thomas Hensman, a labourer, was branded for stealing twenty three sheep and four lambs from a field at Keysoe. He confessed to driving them to Oundle in Northamptonshire and selling them in the market for about 12 shillings each. But his Keysoe neighbours became suspicions when he reappeared and laid out 'much money in household stuffe' which they doubted he could have earned honestly. The brandmark was a trouble to the thief; one fellmonger became suspicious when a man offered him a sheepskin with the markings cut out. Six men got together at Marston Moretaine, stole a sheep from a field and took it to an alehouse to have a meal, but the landlady made them dress and cook it themselves. Afterwards she 'heard a whisperinge amongst them concerning what should become of the shepskin and one ... said putt stones into it and sink it in the brooke'. The theft of other livestock, such as cows, chickens, geese and on one occasion a hive of bees, is also recorded.

POACHING

A yeoman and a miller of Barton were to appear at the Winter Assizes in 1662 on a charge of stealing deer from Wrest Park, the seat of the Countess of Kent, but there is no further evidence of this case. In 1666 the case against two men of Houghton Conquest for hunting with greyhounds and taking three does in Bury Park was dismissed. Three years later a poacher was killed in a fight with two gamekeepers in Ampthill warren. The gamekeepers going their rounds at four in the morning came upon a 'hay' or net set to catch rabbits. As they were removing it two poachers, Ambrose Whittamore and Williams Evans, fell upon them, and in the fight that followed Whittamore was fatally wounded. Evans made his escape. The gamekeepers reported that they had taken Whittamore's body to the 'Bell' at Ampthill, together with the 'hay' and a long staff as evidence for the constable. In 1683 as many as four presentments were brought against George Sole of Flitwick, the man who appeared at the Assizes in 1679 on a charge of consorting with highwaymen. This time he was accused of poaching in the warrens at Woburn,and at Millbrook, of 'riotously assembling with swords and sticks at night' and breaking into Woburn Park together with another man, and of unlawfully keeping a greyhound. A servant of the Earl of Bedford gave evidence that he had been coming home at midnight with some other servants, and had found four horses tied up to a hedge near the Park. They had secured the horses in a stable, and had lain in wait until three o'clock in the morning for their owners. At length five men including George Sole came out of the lane. One of them dropped a bundle of staves used for 'pitching a net to catch deer', and they had a greyhound with them. Sole in evidence confessed to catching rabbits at Woburn and Millbrook, but denied the more serious charge of stealing deer. Rather surprisingly, the jury found there was no case against him on any of the charges. The other men seem to have escaped altogether,

ROGUES AND VAGABONDS

The Assize records give a vivid picture of seventeenth century rogues and vagabonds, people who roamed the countryside, unable or unwilling to find work, in spite of the Elizabethan Poor Laws by which the parish overseers were responsible for making the able-bodied work and in spite of the Act of Settlement of 1662. This enacted that forty day's residence constituted a settlement; as a result every overseer tried to prevent labourers from coming to live in his parish, lest they might become chargeable' to it in the future. At the Winter Assizes in 1680 two vagrants, Richard Knight and Ellis 'his pretended wife' who called herself a lace-buyer, were charged with sheepstealing, on the evidence of an unemployed blacksmith whom they had hired as a drover, but who had backed out when he saw them pick sheep from a flock grazing on Winslow cannon in Buckinghamshire. 'it happening to thunder and lighten very much that night (he) left them perceiving their purpose'. Richard and Ellis spent the night on the common. The blacksmith said that Ellis had told her that 'she had gone two yeares about the country a mumping (as she called it) with a pretended husband who feigned himselfe dumbe ' .

Fairs and markets attracted the vagabond. A baker of Leighton Buzzard told the justices in 1671 that he had seen a pickpocket, Daniel Roberte, plying his trade successively at Woburn Aylesbury and Leighton markets, and at Aylesbury 'he told him he came there for no good. And withall gave him some blows with his whip*. Roberte*s story was that he had only just arrived from Leeds, travelling to London to get himself a place, and that from Doncaster he had helped a drover for 2d. a day and meat. Several people who had come from London were arrested for acting suspiciously at Elstow fair in May 1675. Three women arrived at the fair wearing hats, but had later gone into a house and had reappeared wearing hoods. The daughter of the house thought they were pickpockets. One of the women said that she had come from Southwark, and travelled about buying hair. A man arrested, Robert, Banser, had been seen coming out of a room in John Whitbread's house where money was stored in a chest, for the convenience of traders and in the care of 'a hyred tender for the fayre time', who came under suspicion himself when £117 was found stolen. However, Banser and his brother were found not guilty at the Assizes.

Old or unemployed soldiers and sailors might become vagrants. In 1681 Christopher Gunhus, sentenced at the Assizes to be whipped for the theft of a pile of birch besoms, told the justices that he travelled around mending chair-bottoms, and had been 'one of the late rayised Army under the command of Sir Thomas Slingsby ... in the County of Yorke'. This was a regiment of foot raised in 1678 by the former Governor of Scarborough Castle. It had served in Flanders the same year. Evidence against Gunhus was that he had begged a night's shelter from the constable of Great Barford by pretending to be a lame seaman, and had then stolen the besoms from the barn. John Read and John Clarke, convicted of stealing bacon from a house at Oakley in 1680, were seamen who had left their ships at Yarmouth, arid were travelling home to Stratford-on-Avon. Clarke said he had been whipped as a rogue by the constable of Bury. At Newmarket they had worked for an ostler at the Red Lion, but had left because he would only pay them 2d. a day.

This description of rogues at the Bedfordshire Assizes would be incomplete without mention of the Aman family, whose scandalous behaviour drove the parishioners of Ridgmont to petition the justices in 1680. John Aman, a labourer his wife Ann or Hannah and his daughter, also called Ann or

Hannah, who married John Bland, first appear in the Assize records in 1672, on a charge of receiving stolen goods. In spite of the evidence of Isaac Aman, aged nine, against father and sister, the Amans were found not guilty.

A few years later the mother and daughter were accused of causing the death of an illegitimate child boarded out with them. When Hannah Aman senior had refused to look after the child any longer 'for so little allowance' her daughter had taken it and abandoned it in a field at Edlesborough. She was discovered by the parish overseers who made her take it back, but not surprisingly it died soon after, and the two Hannahs, and the child's father were indicted at the Assizes, The jury, however,found them not guilty. Two years later comes the parishioners complaint. It begins:

'they humble shew that the said Town of Ridgmont bath bin continually troubled with the persons abovenamed for theis Twenty yeares fk upwards besides the charges and damages that they have re ceived -by them continually in Playing the Roague stealing what they could git or lay their hands on by night or by day.

First they steale the saintsbell out of the steeple and sold it. And also stoale A great part of the viceridge house they also have stoale hooks and chains and Iron worke About Gates And also are Notorious for stealing henns and wood out of mens yards in the night'.

They complain of Hannah the daughter for having children which were a charge to the parish. The family harbours rogues and vagabonds, and sells stolen goods. The children are brought up to thieving and never allowed to go into service.

'... they have bin taking wandering sixteen or seventeen weeks together with fasle passes and have made theif brags how well they have lived and bin maintained and carried from place to place their daughter that is now in Gaole when she was A great way of fained herself verey Ill and not Able to goe nor ride in A cart or horse backe and was carried in A Chair on mens shoulders with coltstaffes from place to place till shee came neare hom then shee made he.T escape by Running Away'.

The family have gone to several noblemen's houses with false petitions pretending great losses, and they are also suspected of setting fire to two houses, for which they now await trial in prison.

The first and only page of this amazing account ends at this point. No record remains to show whether the Amans stood trial for arson in 1680, or what became of them afterwards.

INSULTS

It was a great insult to call a man a rogue; and might lead to blows; a Shefford tailor tried to bring an action against a labourer for assault and theft in 1668, but the labourer said the tailor had started the fight by riding up to him crying 'Forsworne Rogue are you not hanged yet' . In 1682 John Warner, gentleman, was indicted for saying to the constable of Wilshamstead 'You are a rogue and I will make you fly the town'. At the same Assizes Oliver Spicer, barber and constable of Shefford, prosecuted two men he had arrested in Shefford market as pickpockets, for 'abusing him in his office as Constable'. He had tried to put them in the stocks 'believing them to be dangerous Rogues and full of beare', but they resisted, and one tried to get his foot out of the stocks, and in doing so 'pulld of his shooe and out of it dropt a good deale of money...'

Later, on their way to the Justice of the Peace, they again tried to escape from their guards. To insult a justice of the peace was worse. A merchant of Ridgmont was indicted at the Assizes in 1683 for saying to Thomas Snagg, *Youi are a foole a Fopp and not fit to be a Justice of fche Peace. And I will have you out of your office within six months'. The sentence passed here is not recorded. In 1683 Edward Sounders was to be prosecuted for speaking 'severall slanderous and scandalous words of his royall highness James Duke of Yorke', the future James II, but there is no evidence of what charge he was indicted. At the Assizes in 1685 a tailor of Bedford was to answer for 'speaking some words relating to the late Duke of Monmouth'. A Biggleswade innholder spoke seditious words, against the King's soldiers in 1679, and was indicted upon complaint of a lieutenant-colonel and a captain in Col. Sir Charles Wheeler's regiment.

CIVIL CASES

In the seventeenth century minor offences might be dealt with at the Assizes, as well as at Quarter Sessions, probably depending on which court happened to be held next. An alehouse keeper might be brought before the Assize judges on a charge of keeping a disorderly house, or for selling ale without a licence. Other people were indicted for such offences as building a cottage without the legal minimum of four acres of land needed to supply food to support the occupants, erecting a dovehouse 'not being the Lord of the Manor nor the Rector of the Parish church', being a common drunkard, a common quarre Her or a common blasphemer. In 1663 a shoemaker of Woburn was indicted for eavesdropping. Each parish was responsible for the upkeep of its own roads and bridges and might be ordered at the Assizes to carry out repairs. There are indictments for putting carrion on the highway, for failing to scour ditches and for digging gravel pits in the highway. Local officers such as constables and surveyors of highways could be indicted for failing to carry out their duties.

NONCONFORMITY AND RECUSANCY

Conformity to the Church of England was again enforced by law after the restoration of the Stuart monarchy in 1669, but for two important intervals, 1672-3 and 1687-9, a policy of toleration for Nonconformist and Catholic alike was attempted. Evidence of the working of the penal laws against Nonconformity in Bedfordshire appears in the Assize records. Indictments for failure to attend church are common.

Five Quakers of Turvey were indicted in 1663, Later evidence of Bedfordshire Quakers occurs in 1685, when a calendar of prisoners records twenty five of them, including a number 'taken on the highway near unto their meeting house and committed as rioters'. In 1666 five Anabaptists were tried for another offence, holding a conventicle or meeting. They had previously refused to pay fines of 20 shillings and 40 shillings. imposed by the local justices, and had spent some thirty days in prison. There is no record that they were convicted nor that they suffered the harsh sentence of banishment decreed for the third offence. Two other Nonconformists, John Dunne and Thomas Haynes, sentenced to exile before 1668, were merely kept in the County Gaol for several years until freed by the Declaration of Indulgence of 1672. It is likely that there was much sympathy for Nonconformists in the county; Sir Matthew Hale was known for his tenderness toward them. He was the judge who had shown pity to John Bunyan' s wife Elizabeth when she came to plead against the sentence of imprisonment imposed on her husband at a Quarter Sessions in 1660, for his refusal to give up preaching.

Bunyan held he had been wrongly convicted, and tried without success to obtain a fresh trial at the Assizes. He remained in the County Gaol until 1672, and his name appears on several gaol calendars. A sympathetic gaoler allowed him some liberty, and he was appointed pastor of the Independent Church in Bedford, later known as the

Bunyan Meeting while still in prison, Another of the church's pastors, Samuel Fenn, was prosecuted at the Assizes in 1669 for saying that the King was not the Governor of the Church of England, but his case was dismissed. The following year twenty eight members of the congregation were arrested at a meeting at John Fenn's house. Nehemiah Cox, later appointed pastor, was 'speaker or teacher' , and at the Winter Assizes in 1671 he was sentenced to remain in prison until he found good sureties, for uttering seditious words. He had told the Justice of the Peace on being questioned that 'the Church of England as it now stands is and anti-Christian church'. He was fined 4 shilling and discharged from gaol at the Summer Assizes. In 1672 Charles II issued his Declaration of Indulgence suspending the penal laws against Nonconformists and Catholics. Before the reimposition of these laws the following year twenty five licences to hold Dissenters' meetings were issued in Bedfordshire.

CONCLUSION

Any conclusion can only be tentative.

If the surviving documents give a true indication theft (including horse and sheep stealing) was six times as frequent as any other kind of crime (60%). House and shopbreaking, and murder and manslaughter, the next largest groups, form together over 20% of the total. The remainder is made up of assault, highway robbery, picking pockets, poaching, receiving, helping prisoners to escape, witchcraft,, coining, arson, rape, assault with theft, receiving bribes.neglect of office, seditious words, slander, forgery, perjury, buggery, uttering arid vending false money, consorting with thieves and consorting with highwaymen. For a population estimated at 40,000 a total of approximately four hundred criminal presentments does not seem excessive. It is hard to say how much has been lost, or how efficient was the administration of justice without a professional police force. To a further question: was the law unduly harsh? again no certain answer can be given. Sometimes it was indeed harsh, but often its theoretical severity was mitigated in practice.

www.ingramcontent.com/pod-product-compliance
Lightning Source LLC
Chambersburg PA
CBHW060604030426
42337CB00019B/3606